The Guic

The Guide was originally produced by the Peddars W inaugural meeting in Swaffham on 14th November objectives:-

1. To press for official designation and completion of the footpath.
2. To promote and publicise the use of the route and its amenities for the benefit of walkers and cyclists.
3. To promote a body of informed opinion that will improve the enjoyment and knowledge of Peddars Way.

As these original objectives appeared to have been achieved and maintenance of the Guide and Accommodation list seemed to be the remaining work, the Peddars Way Association was wound-up at a meeting of members at Dereham on 23rd March 1996, it was agreed that all the assets of the Association should be transferred to the Norfolk Area of the Ramblers' Association, which would continue to edit, publish and distribute the guide book.

The guide is intended to help you plan a holiday or just a day's walk on part of the track and has been kept as simple and inexpensive as possible. The route is described by means of twelve maps, the first seven of which should be read from bottom to top, and the last five from top to bottom. The maps are not fully to scale, but an indication of distance is shown on each sheet. Additional text is there to help you through the trickier sections. There is a separate list to help with accommodation, public transport and places of interest.

If you discover anything needing correction or additional information that would improve the guide, we would like to hear from you, the Guide Editor's address is below.

The Ordnance Survey Landranger maps (1:50,000) numbers 144, 132, 133 and 134 are recommended for the extra detail and information they contain. Even more detail is in the new Explorer maps (1:25000) 229, 236, 250, 251, 252 and Outdoor Leisure map 40.

GUIDE EDITOR	Ian Mitchell	Telephone 01603 622539
	5, Montcalm Road, Norwich, NR1 4HX	
DISTRIBUTION	Sheila Smith, Caldcleugh, Old Buckenham,	E-mail: sheilasmith@clara.co.uk
	Attleborough, Norfolk, NR17 1RU	Telephone 01953 861094

ACKNOWLEDGEMENTS:

Original maps and route descriptions by Alan & Penny Jenyon.
Ian Smith & Colin Hills.
Accommodation list by Ian Mitchell, John Kent & Derek Goddard
Computer layout by Sheila Smith.

Published by: The Ramblers Association, Norfolk Area

Copyright: The Ramblers Association

35th Edition. Revised and reprinted annually. February, 2003

Introduction

A guide to a route of 149 miles (239 kilometres), showing the surprising variety of Norfolk scenery from Knettishall Heath on the Suffolk border to Great Yarmouth.

The **PEDDARS WAY** is an ancient track, mainly Roman in the form in which we see today, but probably pre-Roman in origin. The original route may have run from Colchester to Lincolnshire, with a ferry or ford over the Wash. Peddars Way certainly contributed to the downfall of Queen Boadicea and the Iceni tribes. The surviving part of the route stretches from Knettishall Heath near Thetford in the south, to the coast at Holme. The Secretary of State for the Environment approved the Countryside Commission's proposals in Oct.1982 for a long distance route of 93 miles (149kms) to be known as **THE PEDDARS WAY and NORFOLK COAST PATH.**

THE FOOTPATH WAS OFFICIALLY OPENED on JULY 8th 1986 by

HRH. PRINCE CHARLES.

The **WEAVERS WAY** footpath, from Cromer to Gt. Yarmouth, devised by Norfolk County Council has been included in this guide as a continuation of the long distance path and adding another 56 miles (90kms).

A further route called the **ANGLES WAY** has been created by Norfolk & Suffolk County Councils, to link the Weavers Way at Yarmouth to the Peddars Way at Knettishall Heath, thus creating a circular route of 226 miles (362kms).

TABLE OF DISTANCES	miles	kilometres
PEDDARS WAY	47	75
NORFOLK COAST PATH	46	74
Long Distance Path Total	93	149
WEAVERS WAY	56	90
Total covered in Guide	149	239
ANGLES WAY	77	123
Total "Round Norfolk"	226	362

ICENI WAY - A walk from Knettishall Heath via Thetford & Brandon along the banks of the Little & Great Ouse to Kings Lynn and via Sandringham to Hunstanton. This includes a 15mile (24kms) off-road route between Knettishall Heath and Thetford. The Iceni Way and Peddars Way together can provide a 130mile (210km) circuit with easier transport links.

Guides & accommodation lists for the Angles Way and the Iceni Way are available from Ramblers Association, Sheila Smith, Caldcleugh, Cake Street, Old Buckenham, Attleborough, NR17 1RU. The Angles Way Guide costs £3.00, the Iceni Way Guide costs £2.40, both including post and packing.

A cloth badge, to commemorate your journey along the Peddars Way and Norfolk Coast path, is available in return for your comments. Contact The National Trail Office, Baron's Close, Fakenham, Norfolk, NR21 8BE for details. Email: nationaltrail@norfolk.gov.uk. Tel: 01328 85053

Peddars Way & Norfolk Coast Path

Symbols used on maps

- Major roads
- Minor roads
- Tracks
- Footpaths

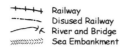
- Railway
- Disused Railway
- River and Bridge
- Sea Embankment

- Church
- Windmill/windpump
- Youth Hostel
- C Camping
- BK Bunk Barn

- S Shop
- PH Public House
- R Refreshments
- PC Toilets
- P Car park

Until reaching point 8 the maps should be read from the bottom working upwards.

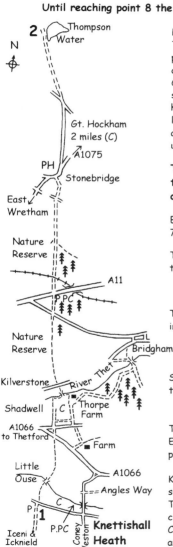

Breckland is the unique region of heathland crossed by Peddars Way. The soil is sandy, dry and infertile, partly due to the Neolithic farming practice of 'slash and burn', crops are prone to drought in a dry summer and much of the area has been planted with conifers by the Forestry Commission. Something of the original character of the area can be seen approaching Thompson Water with Scots pine scattered on open heath. There are several Breckland 'meres' which have higher water levels in summer than in winter! Thompson Water, however, is an artificial lake dug out in the 19th century and more recently has been used for trout farming.

This section of the route passes through the Stanford battle training area. Do not stray from the path because of the danger from unexploded shells.

East Wretham Heath, Norfolk Wildlife Trust Reserve: T. 01842 755010.

This section of Peddars Way is at its finest in Spring when the May trees are in bloom.

There is a nature reserve here maintained by the Nature Conservancy in order to preserve some of the traditional Breckland.

Shadwell is named after Chad's well, a shrine for pilgrims. The church tower has been buttressed for over 600 years but still stands strong.

Thetford, meaning 'the people's ford' was the capital of Anglo-Saxon England in King Canute's time. Castle Hill earthworks, 800 year old priory and Ancient House Museum (archaeology) open daily.

Knettishall Heath Country Park preserves some traditional Breckland scenery and is a centre for serious ramblers and gentle strollers. The Angles Way is a 78 mile route to Great Yarmouth, the Icknield Way connects with The Ridgeway and the Iceni Way joins the Norfolk Coastal Path at Hunstanton following an 80 mile Breck and Fenland route around south and west Norfolk. There are also numerous footpaths across the Heath for short rambles.

(9 miles [15km] approx. 1-2)

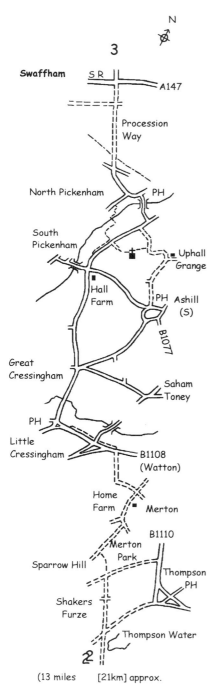

Swaffham is an old market town with a lively Saturday market: auctions of bric-a-brac, farm produce, cars and livestock. The village sign recalls the legend of the pedlar of Swaffham. The fine 15th century church has a splendid double hammer-beam roof, with 150 angels carved 500 years ago.

Access to the Peddars Way from the south-east edge of Swaffham is off the North Pickenham Road by a steep vehicle track eastward, indicated by a metal signpost. Procession Way is reached after one mile along this track

Procession Way derives its name from the regular religious processions which used it in medieval times.

On the hill towards Uphall Grange is the recently restored St. Mary's Church, Houghton-on-the-Hill, where 10th or 11th century wall paintings were found.

South Pickenham Hall to your left is a fine example of a country house built in the neo-Georgian style in 1902 - 05. There is a round tower church nearby.

Great Cressingham is an old village with thatched cottages and a fine 14th century church, with some fine brasses and memories of Cromwell's time.

Watton is an old town with a Norman church and 14th century belfry. Nearby is Wayland Wood or 'wailing wood' - the place of the legend 'Babes in the Wood'.

North of Home Farm a bridleway leading straight on reaches B1108 on the western edge of Watton, from there a bridleway and road leads to Saham Toney.

Merton, originally 'mere town', has Roman connections. It has a fine 13th century church.

On reaching Sparrow Hill go on northwards in the fenced section at the edge of the battle area. This joins a track which enters Merton Park in which you continue due north, finally coming out onto the track which passes Home Farm.

The village of Thompson existed before the conquest and the church is one the best examples to be found in Norfolk of the early decorated period - 14th century.

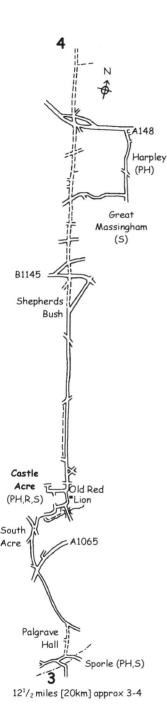

Several good examples of tumuli - ancient burial mounds - can be seen on this stretch of the route.

Great Massingham is noted for the size of the village pond. Nearby is a fine 14th century church with a pinnacled tower and remains of an 11th century priory.

Shepherds Bush is one of the highest points on the Norfolk stretch of the Peddars Way. Another Roman road, from Brisley to King's Lynn, may have crossed the route about here.

Notice the change in scenery from the infertile Breckland in the south to the highly cultivated rolling hills of west Norfolk.

Castle Acre has Roman, Saxon and Norman connections. The tall gateway opening onto the village green was a gate of the castle in Norman times. The castle hill is on the site of the Roman camp, one of the biggest East Anglian fortresses of the day. A Roman road, from Denver to Smallburgh once crossed west to east just south of the town.

The Norman Priory can be seen from the road by South Acre. It stands next to the river which the monks used to supply fishponds in the priory grounds. The buildings and foundations cover 36 acres. Access is from the street west of the church.

12½ miles [20km] approx 3-4

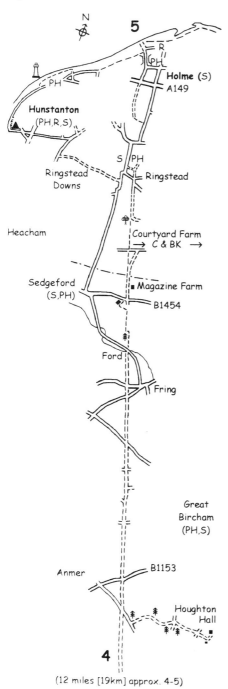

Hunstanton its heyday in the Victorian railway era - the line is now closed. On clear evenings you can watch the sun setting over the sea. The cliffs are striped red and white with carrstone and chalk and Fulmars breed here.

The carrstone is quarried locally and can be seen in many local buildings, although it is not particularly durable.

Ringstead Downs is a chalkland valley, unusual in Norfolk. **This is a quick way into Hunstanton if needed. (3 miles or 5km.)**

North of the disused railway, follow Peddars Way across the field or use the farm track just to the east - both are rights of way. The Peddars Way continues along the west side of the hedge, up the hill towards Ringstead.

North of the Fring to Sedgeford Road, stay east of the hedge until you reach a small wood. A little further on is a sign taking you to the west side of the hedge. Follow signs on a diversion around a field as you approach the B1454.

Fring has a 14th century church with its belfry windows still intact.

Sandringham (off the route) house, gardens, museum and nature trail. Open Sunday to Thursday, April to September - but closed on special occasions.

Anmer, a village on the Sandringham estate, with a fine church and 16th century Hall.

Houghton Hall built by Sir Robert Walpole, the first Prime Minister of England. There is a large collection of model soldiers. Open Easter to September, Sundays, Thursdays and Bank holidays. 2.30 - 5.30 pm. (T. 01485 528569)

(12 miles [19km] approx. 4-5)

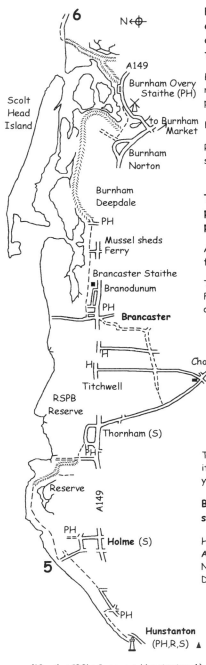

From Burnham Overy Staithe go along the sea bank, eventually reaching the beach. The right of way is along the beach. In May, June and July walk below the high tide line to avoid nesting terns.

Burnham Thorpe (two miles inland) - Nelson's birthplace in the rectory has been demolished. A plaque on a wall marks the place.

Ferry runs from the Staithe to Scolt Head in summer months.

Remains of St. Mary's Carmelite Friary, founded 1241, are situated between Burnham Market and Burnham Overy Town.

The path from the mussel sheds follows the bank top past the houses, you may walk on the marsh if you prefer.

A ferry leaves from Brancaster Staithe in the summer months for Scolt Head National Reserve (tern colonies).

The LDP passes Branodunum the site of one of three Roman Forts on the Norfolk coast. Dalmatian cavalry under "The Count of the Saxon Shore" dealt with invaders from the Continent.

Between Thornham and Brancaster there is no safe route to the seaward side of the A149, nor is there a footpath beside the main road for those wishing to visit the RSPB Reserve, or who have accommodation in Titchwell. To avoid this busy road it is necessary to divert inland nearly as far as Choseley Farm, but the views are outstanding.

Thornham, formerly famous for its forge, is worth visiting for its 17th century manor house and 14th century church with 500 year old screens.

Between Holme and Thornham observe any diversion signs seen, as the path is subject to erosion.

Holme Bird Observatory is run by the Norfolk Ornithologists' Association and is famous for sightings of migratory birds. Nearby is the Norfolk Wildlife Trust reserve and nature trail. Details: The Firs, Broadwater Road, Holme. Tel: 01485 552240

From Hunstanton go to the lighthouse then along the cliff footpath and behind the le Strange Hotel, turn inland, then after a short way go northeast again along links road, past the club house and skirt south side of golf links to reach Holme via the beach road.

(19 miles [30km] approx. Hunstanton-6)

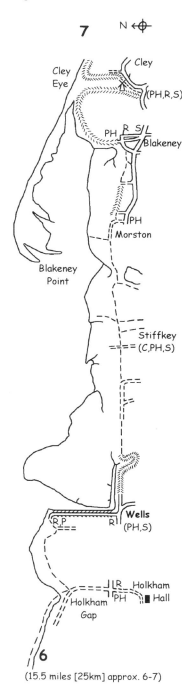

Glandford Shell Museum (2 miles south from Cley), by the Church - a world-wide collection. Also Tapestry of the Norfolk coast. Open from March to October. Tuesday to Saturday and Bank holidays. 10 - 12.30, 2 - 4.30. GR: 044414.

From Blakeney, go seawards on the sea wall and cross the River Glaven at the sluice next to A149. Continue to Cley High Street. Turn left along the busy street, but soon turn left to the sea wall and turn right to Cley Mill. Pass to the right of the mill and follow the sea bank to the coastguard station at Cley Eye.

Blakeney used to be a great seaport, provisioning the tall ships used in the crusades. Now the harbour is silted up, the only boats are small pleasure craft and a few passenger ferries making trips to view the seals and land at Blakeney Point in the summer. Ferry also from Morston to Blakeney Point in the summer months.

Saltmarshes are a characteristic of this part of the coast and are a wintering and breeding area for birds. Most of this coast has been purchased by conservation bodies, mainly the National Trust. The plants are specially adapted to withstand occasional inundation by seawater. One of these plants provides the local delicacy "samphire".

Stiffkey famous for its cockles (Stewkey Blues) which are commemorated on the village sign.

Be careful if you go seawards over the marsh and sand-flats. It is easy to lose your way and be cut-off by a rising tide.

Wells is the only port left on the North Norfolk coast with a usable harbour and is occasionally used for the movement of grain and fertilizer. A number of fishing and pleasure craft moor here.

Holkham Hall the 18th century home of the Earls of Leicester. (Coke of Norfolk became famous for his Norfolk Rotation and other pioneering agricultural methods). Hall (tapestries and pictures) and Bygones Museum open 1 - 5 pm Sunday - Thursday, June to September and 11.30 - 5pm Sunday and Monday Easter, Spring and Summer Bank holidays. Normally there is all year access to the park walks (fallow deer and bird life).

Holkham pines planted to stop the sand dunes from moving inland, so that the marshes could be reclaimed.

Go along the beach until you reach the board walk at Holkham Gap, then go inland of the woods and turn eastwards along the track between the woods and the marsh. Go onto the top of the sea bank for the approach to Wells.

(15.5 miles [25km] approx. 6-7)

The Cromer Ridge, which is the high ground inland of the town is evidence of glaciation during the ice ages.

Cromer is famous for crab fishing. Sea defences attempt to control the erosion of the cliffs, a problem on this part of the coast. The church tower is the highest in Norfolk after Norwich Cathedral.

Felbrigg Hall a 17th century house with original 18th century furniture. Walled garden, tea shop. National Trust, open April to October. Saturday to Wednesday 1 pm - 5pm

Leave Sheringham by the sea-front and take the path over Beeston Hump along the cliff. Turn right, following the left edge of a field, over the level crossing and across the main road. Go past Beeston Hall and after a sharp turn left at the bottom of the hill, fork right and go up towards Beacon Hill and Roman Camp. Go over the road and bear left into a footpath in front of a gate. Go down through the wood as far as the Camping Club site, then turn right onto a path, go over Abbs Common and into a green lane. Continue under the railway bridge to reach Cromer.

Sheringham Park is known for its exotic plants and Rhododendron Woods. Grounds open all the year (NT), there is a fine view of the coast from the Gazebo.

On the cliff edge route into Sheringham be wary of the cliffs and golfers.

North Norfolk Railway, Sheringham - Weybourne - High Kelling. Steam trains on summer weekends and bank holidays.

'He that would olde Englande win
Should at Weybourne Hope begin.'
(deep water close to the shore would have been of help to an invasion).

Beyond the redundant radar station the sight and sound of old military vehicles comes from the Muckleburgh Collection. Entrance on main road GR: 105428.

East of Gramborough hill the walking becomes easier.

Follow the shingle bank, on top or either side. This is remounded mechanically, possibly several times every winter. In February 1996 it was washed over and the salt water flooded the nature reserve. **Mines placed on the beach during the 1939-45 War occasionally reappear, keep a lookout. Bathing is not safe in this area anyway.**

Norfolk Wildlife Trust Information Centre with an exhibition about the North Norfolk Coast is the thatched cottage just east of Cley.

(12 miles [19km] approx. 7- Cromer)

Weavers Way

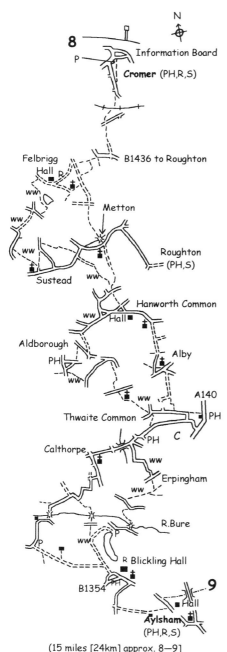

(15 miles [24km] approx. 8—9)

You may now set off on the Weavers Way which is a route developed and published by the Norfolk County Council. It is 56 miles from Cromer to Great Yarmouth. The route was revised in 1997.

The following maps are based on the information in a leaflet which is available from: Planning & Transportation, County Hall, Martineau Lane, Norwich, NR1 2DH and local tourist information centres.

The current route is waymarked with disks on posts, and is shown with "WW" on this map. The previous route is also shown here as it appears on the Explorer Map, published early in 1997.

Eastern Norfolk has a concentration of round tower churches. There are very few in the country outside Norfolk and Suffolk. W.J. Goode, in his book 'Round Tower Churches of South East England' argues that the construction of many of them is Saxon, dating from as early as 800 AD.

Round tower - St. Peter & St. Paul, Sustead.

St Bartholomew's Church at Hanworth dates from the 14th- 15th century and has fine medieval workmanship.

Round tower - All Saints Church, Thwaite.

Thwaite common, an area of semi-natural grassland which, although privately owned, has rights of pasture over it.

St Margaret's Church, Calthorpe, mainly dates from the 13th century.

Blickling Hall was built 1616-27. One of the most impressive Jacobean houses in England, now owned by the National Trust. The house is open during the season: April to October 1pm - 4.30pm Wednesday to Sunday plus Bank Holiday Mondays. Also Tuesdays in August. Garden as above from 10.30 am. The path around the lake is open at any time.

St. Andrews Church, Blickling, has a number of brasses.

Aylsham was an important medieval centre for the manufacture of fine linen cloth called Aylsham Webb. It is still a thriving market town.

Most of the route of this map follows the disused track of the former Midland and Great Northern railway line from King's Lynn to Great Yarmouth. (the sections not following the track are well signposted.

The line was closed in 1959 and since then a pleasing variety of trees, shrubs and wildflowers have colonised the route making a very attractive path and bridleway.

Those wishing to avoid North Walsham may use the signposted official diversion to Meeting House Hill.

This route crosses a battlefield of 1381 during the Peasants Revolt.

North Walsham was another important medieval centre for the weaving industry of the area, with an important market for both wool and finished cloth. Today it is still a market town with considerable industry.

Go through the town centre past the market cross and leave by the Old Yarmouth Road, follow the footpath and go left into the minor road. At the crossroads turn right into Holgate lane then go first left, first right, to Meeting House Hill.

Turn right to a footpath then left across the field back to the disused railway just before the bypass.

The village of Worstead, a few miles off the route, from Bengate, gave its name to worstead cloth. This village was extremely wealthy when the wool industry was at its height, as shown by the size of the church. Today it is a small though attractive village.

North Walsham and Dilham Canal was built in the early 19th century to bring coal into North Walsham and goods out, but never a commercial success.

10 (14 miles [23km] approx. 9-10

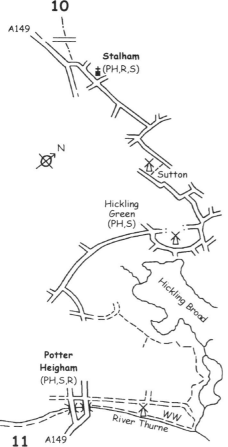

The final section of The Weavers' Way from Stalham to Great Yarmouth is a further 27 miles (43km).

The route includes extensive Broadland riverside stretches with wide views over open valley land and marshes. There is a striking contrast between the traditional undrained marshland around Hickling Broad and the newly drained agricultural land of the lower Bure and Yare. Many old windpumps formerly used for drainage are notable landmarks.

Stalham, now a holiday centre on the edge of the Broads, has long been a centre for the surrounding countryside: wherries plied between here and Great Yarmouth.

The Way first follows minor country roads but takes a footpath past Sutton Windmill — the tallest surviving mill in the country with all machinery still in place.

Hickling Broad national nature reserve covers 1200 acres (485 hectares), including all Hickling Broad and Heigham Sound. Surrounded by reed beds and fen, it is an important habitat for breeding and over-wintering birds. **Please take extra care to protect the wildlife.**

From the nature reserve entrance to Acle most of the way is along river banks. It skirts the south edge of Hickling Broad and side of Heigham Sound. South of Potter Heigham it follows the Thurne and Bure.

(10 miles [16km] approx. 10-11)

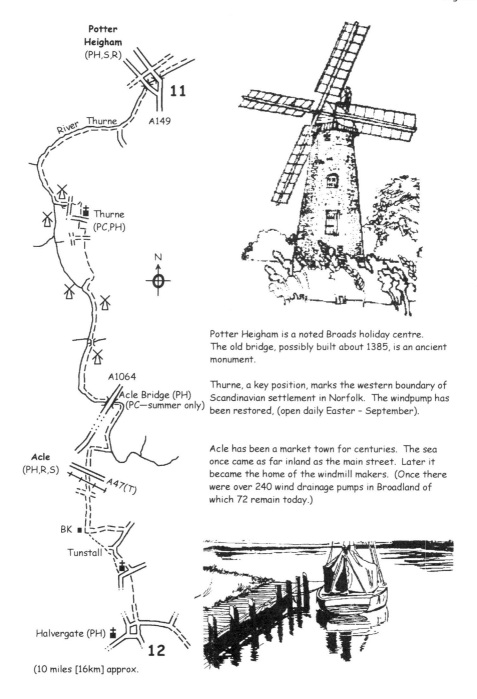

Potter Heigham is a noted Broads holiday centre. The old bridge, possibly built about 1385, is an ancient monument.

Thurne, a key position, marks the western boundary of Scandinavian settlement in Norfolk. The windpump has been restored, (open daily Easter – September).

Acle has been a market town for centuries. The sea once came as far inland as the main street. Later it became the home of the windmill makers. (Once there were over 240 wind drainage pumps in Broadland of which 72 remain today.)

(10 miles [16km] approx.

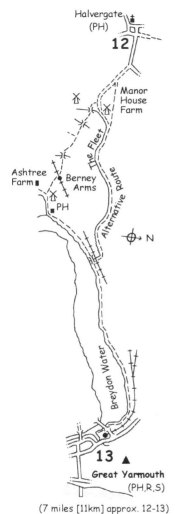

The way now crosses low-lying farmland and grazing marshes, some of the largest and most important in the country. Paths often remain boggy till May – boots advised.

The path follows the old marsh road to Manor House Farm, then across the marshes to the Berney Arms to join the path along Breydon Wall and Breydon Sluice. (Please close gates.)

Berney Arms windpump is an ancient monument dating from 1870 (open April—September but times vary).

Breydon Water, a local nature reserve, is important for migrating birds especially waders and wildfowl. Boats raised on stilts are observation huts.

The way follows the flood wall on the north Bank of Breydon Water to Great Yarmouth. Pass Vauxhall Station, continue via North Quay and Market Place to the Tourist Information Centre near Britannia Pier.

Great Yarmouth was built on a sandbar that shifted many times and led to a constant medieval battle to keep the harbour open. The town developed as a fishing port, becoming a popular holiday resort in the 19th century. The old commercial centre faces the harbour and the "new" town of hotels, boarding houses and entertainments faces the sea.

(7 miles [11km] approx. 12-13)

Transport

TRAINS serving the area are run by Anglia Railways, Central Trains and WAGN. These stations may be useful for getting into the area: On the route: Sheringham, Cromer, North Walsham, Acle, Berney Arms, Great Yarmouth. Others: King's Lynn, Thetford, Bury St. Edmunds, Diss, Norwich. . Information on times and fares from staffed stations and National Rail Enquiries: 08457 48 49 50

BUSES Enquiries to East Anglia Traveline 0870 608 2 608 daily, 8.00 - 20.00.
Bus Information Centre, Castle Meadow, Norwich, Monday- Saturday 8.30 - 17.00

The following regular all year service routes may be useful:

King's Lynn—Swaffham—Norwich	King's Lynn—Hunstanton
King's Lynn—Massingham—Fakenham—Wells	King's Lynn—Swaffham—Watton—Attleborough—Diss
King's Lynn—Fakenham—Sheringham—Cromer	Sheringham—Wells—Hunstanton
Norwich—Aylsham—Cromer—Sheringham	Norwich—North Walsham
Norwich—Acle—Great Yarmouth	Norwich—Fakenham—(Wells on Sunday)
Watton—Dereham—Norwich—Yarmouth—Lowestoft	Norwich—Wymondham—Attleborough—Watton—Ashill
Watton—Thetford (Post-bus)	

Express Bus services between Thetford and Norwich do not stop anywhere near the Peddars Way crossing of the A11.
Coastal Bus Service 36 run by Norfolk Green (T. 01553 776980) daily throughout the year between Hunstanton and Sheringham. Even on winter Sundays there are 3 buses each way and the coast path could be walked in short lengths using this service from a several night stopover. There are connecting services to King's Lynn and Cromer or Norwich.

KNETTISHALL HEATH is 5 miles (8kms) by direct road from Thetford railway station, about half being along the busy A1066. A taxi may be the best solution for a small group to share. The most frequent bus service is from Bury St. Edmunds to Coney Weston, about 2 miles (3kms) to the south by minor road. The journey takes about 50 minutes. Bury St. Edmunds is on the Ipswich - Peterborough rail line.
There is no security for cars at Knettishall Heath and they should not be left there except during a day walk.

Eastern Counties Service 337/8	Mon-Sat	Mon-Fri school days	Mon-Sat	Mon-Sat
Bury St. Edmunds Bus Station	12.35	15.50	17.20	17.50
Coney Weston, Three Cross Ways	13.17	16.45	18.13	18.43

All continue to Hopton and Garboldisham (see Accommodation list)

Return journeys	Mon-Sat	Mon-Sat	Mon-Sat	Mon-Sat	Mon-Sat
Coney Weston, Three Cross Ways	7.30	7.59	9.40	13.40	17.23*
Bury St. Edmunds Bus Station	8.23	8.43	10.23	14.23	17.48

* From Barningham, Royal George (one mile further from Coney Weston)

Pick up service.
Along the southern part of the Peddars Way several guesthouses (some located at a distance from the route) provide a Pick-up Service for those staying with them. Contact them individually to check what arrangements they are able to offer. See accommodation pages 16-20 under the following locations - Barnham, East Harling, Hopton, New Buckenham, Great Hockham, Great Ellingham, Mundford, Stow Bedon, Griston, Watton, Carbrooke, Great Cresssingham, Ashill, Swaffham, Sporle, Wendling, Gressenhall, Narborough and Brisley.

Accommodation

Places providing accommodation within half an hour of the route have been included unless a longer distance is specified. Please let us know of any places that do not meet a reasonable standard or have closed. We should also like to hear of places which are worth including.
An indication is given to some accommodation prices but prices should be checked at time of booking. A premium is sometimes asked for singles, possibly placing them in the next higher price band.

The following towns are known to have more accommodation than we can list, so in case of difficulty their tourist information phone numbers are given:

| Hunstanton | 01485 532610 | Wells | 0870 225 4857 | Sheringham | 0870 225 4854 |
| Cromer | 0870 225 4853 | Swaffham | 01760 722255 | Great Yarmouth | 01493 846345 |

The following abbreviations have been used:

B	Bank/Building Society	S	Shop (Early closing Wednesday if not stated)			£	to £18 a night
R	Refreshments/Meals	C	Campsite or possible camping, eg garden of a pub			£+	£18 to £23
G	Guest House	EM	Evening meal (at guest house always by booking)			£++	£23 to £26
Y	Hostel YHA or other	H	Hotel	D	Double room	T. Telephone	£+++	£26 to £30
PH	Public House	I	Inn	T	Twin room	F. Fax	£++++	£30 or over
BB	Bed & Breakfast	BK	Bunk Barn	F	Family room	Std Telephone area code		
Ecd	Early closing day	PC	Toilets	S	Single room	GR: Grid reference		
PWp	Pick up service by arrangement			#	Location only suitable if combined with pick up service or similar.			

Postal towns, where shown, should not be assumed to have any geographical relevance.

Knettishall Heath Std 01953
For access to Knettishall Heath please see details on previous page.
Car Parking - GR:944807 and GR:956807, but **No Security**.
    C   GR:955807. Please inform Country Park Warden. (T.688265)
    PC   No Shop. Information Office Open At Weekends. GR:955807

Coney Weston Std 01359 2 miles (4kms) by Lane S.E. of Country Park
    PH   Swan, T.221295. Real ale. No food.

Barnham (Thetford) Std 01842 5 miles (8kms) via **Iceni Way** (see page 2) to Euston, then by minor road.
    BB   Mrs. Margaret Heading, East Farm, Euston Road. IP24 2PB. T.890231. F.890457. BB £++ D1, T1.
           Packed lunches by arrangement. PWp.

East Harling (Norwich) Std 01953 5 miles (8kms) by road, 6 miles (9.5kms) by path.
    G   Mrs. Lorna Lynn, The Old Dairy, White Hart Street, NR16 2NE. T.717687. BB £++
          D1, T1, F1 (will adapt to S4). No EM, four eating places in village. PWp. Car parking while away.

Garboldisham (Diss) Std 01953 4 miles (6.5kms) via **Angles Way** (see page 2.)
    G   Jean Stone. Ingleneuk Lodge, Hopton Rd. T.681541. BB £+++ D3, T2, F2, S2. EM

Hopton (Diss) Std 01953 4 miles (6.5kms) via **Angles Way** (see page 2.)
    G   Sue & Tony Tomlinson, Hollybank, High Street, IP22 2QX. T.688147. BB D2, T1.
          Willing to transport to/from Knettishall Heath or bus/rail stations at Thetford or Diss.

New Buckenham (Norwich) Std 01953 #
    G   Pump Court, Church Street, NR16 2BA. T.661039. pumpcourt@lineone.net www.pump-court.co.uk
          BB £+ D1, T1. PWp All year.

Thetford Std 01842. 5 miles (8kms) see notes on Transport.
- PH   Black Horse Inn, GR:873832.   Norfolk Plover, GR:865827.   Red Lion Inn, GR:872830.
- H   Anchor Hotel, Bridge Street. T.763925.   BB.   D8, F2, T1, S5.
- H   Thomas Paine, White Hart Street, IP24 1AA.   T.755631. F.766505.   www.thomaspainehotel.co.uk bookings@thomaspainehotel.co.uk.   BB £+++   D7, T2, S3.
- H   Bell Hotel, King Street, IP24 2AZ.   T.754455.   F.755552.   bell.thetford@oldenglishinns.co.uk   www.oldenglishinns.co.uk   £++++ D15, T15, S12.
- H   Wereham House Hotel, 24, White Hart Street, IP24 1AD. T.761956.   F.765207.   www.werehamhousehotel.co.uk   wereham@flexnet.co.uk   BB £+++   D4, T2, S1
- G   Mrs Findlay, 43 Magdalen Street.   T.764564.   BB £+   T2, S1.
- G   Mrs Dooley, 30 Raymond Street.   T.765419.   BB £+   D1, T1, S2.
- G   Mrs Mason, 4 Raymond Street.   T.754546. BB £+   D3, T2, S1.

Thorpe Woodlands   Std 01842   2 miles (3kms) along Peddars Way on River Thet
- C   Small nightly charge: toilet/washroom, no shower, limited shop. Large parties T.751042 (Forest Enterprises) Easter – September.

West Harling (Norwich) Std 01953
- C   The Dower House Touring Park, East Harling, NR16 2SE.   GR:970852.   T.717314.   F.717843. info@dowerhouse.co.uk   www.dowerhouse.co.uk   80 tents £12 per tent.   March – October

Bridgham   Std 01953   Phone box, no shops.

Bridgham Heath
- PC   GR:936871.   South side of A11.   Refreshment stall at times.

East Wretham   Std 01953.
- C   Mrs. Hazelby, Larkshall House, East Wretham.   GR:917890.   T.498347.

Stonebridge,   East Wretham (on A1075)   Std 01953
- PH   Brian Ashman, Dog & Partridge, Watton Road, IP24 1QS.   T.498245   Lunch/EM.
- G   Mr. & Mrs. Barke, Highfields, 2, Windmill Lane, T.498700. Annex for 4.   Horse livery.

Great Hockham (Thetford) Std 01953   1.5 miles (2.4kms)
- PH   The Eagle,   Harling Road,   T.498216.
- G   Manor Farm, Vicarage Road, IP24 1PE   GR:951926.   T./F.498204.   manorfarm@ukf.net BB £+ - £++   D1, T/F1, S1.   EM £6.50 - £16.50.   All year except Xmas. Stabling etc. PWp
- C   Mrs. Rands, Puddledock Farm.   GR:941925.   T.498455.   £3.50 per tent.
- S   The Stores.

Thompson (Thetford) Std 01953   1 mile   (1.6kms)
- I   Mr. & Mrs. McDowell, Chequers Inn, Griston Road IP24 1PX.   T.483360.   F.488092 www.thompsonchequers.co.uk   Real ale. Meals.   BB £++++
- G   Mrs. L. Garnier, College Farm, IP24 1QG.   GR:932967.   T./F.483318.   collegefarm@amserve.net BB £++ D2, T1.   No EM.   All year.
- G   Brenda Mills, Thatched House, Pockthorpe Corner, IP24 1PJ.   GR:918967.   T. 483577.   BB £++ D1, T2.   EM £7.50   7pm.   All year.
- G C   Mr & Mrs. Hornsey, Lands End, Butters Hall Lane, IP24 1QQ. T./F.488070. BB £+   Riding

Great Ellingham (Attleborough) Std 01953 #
- G   Home Cottage Farm, Penhill Road, NR17 1LS.   T.483734.   marshallcraft@hotmail.com £+   Serviced apartment as S, D, T, F or groups.   PWp

Mundford (Thetford) Std 01842 #
- G   Colveston Manor, IP26 5HU. T.878218.   F.879218.   mail@colveston-manor.co.uk www.colveston-manor.co.uk   BB £+   D2, T1, S1.   Stabling, etc.   PWp.

Stow Bedon (Attleborough) Std. 01953 3 miles (5km)
    G   Home Farm, NR17 1BZ. GR:956962. T.483592. F.488449. ejdoveandson@btconnect.co.uk
           BB £++ D1, T1. PWp. Open from Easter 2003

Griston (Watton) Std 01953 3 miles (5km)
    PH   Waggon & Horses, Church Road, meals.
    G   Mrs. D. Ulrych, Park Farm, Caston Road, IP25 6QD. T.483020 F.483056. parkfarm@eidosnet.co.uk
           www.parkfarmbreckland.co.uk BB £+ T1, D1. PWp.
    G   Mrs. J. Garner, Hall Farm, (on A1075) IP25 6QF. T.881626 F.883131 £++

Watton Std 01953 ECD Thursday 1 mile (1.6kms)
    B   Barclays, NatWest, Lloyds/TSB, Norwich & Peterborough.
    H R   Hare & Barrel, 80, Brandon Road, IP25 6LB GR:905007. T.882752. BB £+++
           D4, T7, F1, S6. EM £8 All year. www.hare-and-barrel-hotel-norfolk.co.uk
    H R   The Willow House, 2, High Street, IP25 6AE GR:916008. T.881181. F.885885. www.willowhouse.net
           willowhousewatton@barbox.net BB £+++ D3, T4, S7. PWp.
    H   Crown Hotel, 25, High Street. T.882375. BB £+++ S2, T3, D1. Meals.
    G   Mr. & Mrs. Holman, Orchard House, 55, Griston Road. T.889016, F.889225. BB £++ D1, T1, S1.
    R BB   Richmond Park Golf Club, Saham Road, IP25 6EA. GR:908012. T.881803. £++
    R S   Chinese, Turkish, English take away. Mr. Chips. Somerfield, Tesco Superstore, Londis early-late,

Carbrooke (Watton) Std 01953 #
    G   White Hall, IP25 6SG. T.885950. F.884420. shirleyC30@aol.com BB £++ T1, D2. PWp

Saham Toney (Watton) Std 01953 2 miles (3kms)
    PH   The Bell, Bell Lane. GR:903018. T.884934. Real ale, Food.
    H R   Broom Hall Hotel, Richmond Road, IP25 7EX. GR:903012. T./F.882125. www.broomhallhotel.co.uk
           enquiries@broomhallhotel.co.uk BB £++++ D10, T2, S1.
    G   Cranford House, Ovington Road. GR:912021. T.885292. BB £+++ D2, T1.
           Special BB £++ for walkers/cyclists in Romany wagon in orchard.
    S   Post Office & Stores, Richmond Road. GR: 902019. T.881317

Saham Hills (Watton) Std 01953
    C   Lowe Caravan Park, Ashdale Hills Road, IP25 7EZ. T.881051. Tents from £6 per night.

Little Cressingham (Thetford) Std 01953
    PH   White Horse. GR:873000. T.883434. Real ale. Home cooked food.
    G   Mr. J. Wittridge, Sycamore House, IP25 6NE. T./F.881887. BB £++ D2, T1, S2.
           EM at White Horse across the road. All year.

Great Cressingham (Thetford) Std 01760
    PH   The Windmill Inn, Water End. GR: 845018. T.756232. Real ale. Food
    G   The Vines, The Street, IP25 6NL. GR:849016. T.756303. stay@the.vines.fsbusiness.co.uk
           BB £++ D2, T1. All year. Stabling etc. PWp.

Ashill (Thetford) Std 01760
    PH   White Hart. GR: 886043
    G   Mrs. M. Pickering, Moat Farm, Cressingham Road, IP25 7BX. GR:881034. T.440357. F.441447.
           BB £++ D1, T2. PWp.
    C   Brick Kiln Farm, Swaffham Rd, IP25 7BT. T.441300. brick.kiln@btclick.com All facilities Tents
           £3.70 per night. All year.
    S   Village Stores GR:886042 T.440263 ecd Wed. & Sun.   Stores & P.O. GR:887047. T.440233

South Pickenham Std 01760
    PO   No shop, Post Office only

North Pickenham (Swaffham) Std 01760
- S   Shop & PO, open mornings only . Opposite Blue Lion
- PH   Blue Lion, Hillside. GR:864069. T.440289. Real ale. Bar meals.
- G   Mrs. B.J. Norris, Riverside House, Meadow Lane, PE37 8LE GR:865065. T.440219.
BB £+ T2, D1. Meals at Blue Lion. All year except Xmas

Necton/Swaffham Std 01760
- S R   100m, west of route crossing A47: Garage shop & Macdonalds

Swaffham Std 01760. 2 mile (3kms) Most things are near the Market Place.
- H   George Hotel, Station Rd, PE37 7LJ. GR:820091. T.721238. F.725333 BB £++++ 29 rooms EM.
- H   Horse & Groom, 40 Lynn Street, PE37 7AX. T.721567. F.725542. BB £+++ S6, T5, D6, F2. EM.
- H R   Strattons, 4, Ash Close, PE37 7NH. T.723845. F.720458. strattonshotel@btinternet.com
www.strattons.hotel.co.uk BB £++++   D4, T1
- G   Mrs D. Harvey, Glebe Bungalow, 8a Princes St. PE37 7BP. GR:816089. DoreenMHarvey@aol.com
T.722764. BB £+ D1, T1, All year. PWp.
- G   Mrs C.Webster, Purbeck House, 46 Whitsands Road. PE37 7BJ. GR:815090.
T.721805. BB £+   T2, F2, D2, S2. All year.
- B   H.S.B.C., NatWest, Lloyds T.S.B., Norwich & Peterborough, Nationwide.
- R   Mr Chips, Mother Hubbard's, F.& C., C. Cheng and Hong Kong House Take-Aways.
- R   Romford House Country Restaurant, The Coffee Shop, T Pot Inn, Pedlars Hall Cafe.
- R   Market X Restaurant. T. 724260, Village Tandoori,
- PH   Greyhound. White Hart, Norfolk Hero.
- PH   Red Lion Motel. T.721022. BB £++ D5, T7.
- Taxi   J.B. Taxi Service. T.441273.
- C   Breckland Meadows, Lynn Road. GR:807093. T.721246. F.725994. £5 per tent. March-October

Sporle (Swaffham) Std 01760
- PH   Squirrells Drey. GR:848113. T.724842. Bar Meals, Restaurant Tuesday - Sunday.
- S   Threeway Stores, The Street. GR:849111. T.724300. Ecd Sunday
- S   Newsagent & General Store. GR:849113. Post Office opposite Threeway Stores.
- G   Mrs L.Hickey, Corfield House, The Street, PE32 2EA. GR:849106. T.723636.
corfield.house@virgin.net   www.corfieldhouse.co.uk   BB £++ D2, T2. PWp.
- G   Mr Anderson, Cambridge Cottage. Love Lane, PE32 2EP. GR:844110. T.723718. BB £+ T2.

Wendling (Dereham) Std 01362 #
- H   Greenhanks Country Hotel, Swaffham Road, NR19 2AB. T./F.687742. www.greenbankshotel.co.uk
jenny@greenbankshotel.co.uk BB £++++ T2, D3. PWp

Gressenhall (Dereham) Std 01362 #
- G   Wood Hill, NR19 2NR. T.699186. F.699291. tania.bullard@btopenworld.com BB £++ D2, T1.   PWp

Narborough (King's Lynn) Std 01760 #
- G   Park Cottage, Narford Road, PE32 1HZ. T.337220. BB £   D1, T1, S1. PWp

Castle Acre (King's Lynn) Std 01760
- PH C   Ostrich Inn, Stocks Green. GR:818152. T.755398. Real ale. BB
June - September, T1, F1. Lunch & EM. Possible Camping.
- PH   Albert Victor, Stocks Green. T.756213. Food, BB.
- R S   Castlegate Stores & Restaurant, Stocks Green. Open 7 Days.
- G   Mrs Clarke, Gemini House, Pyes Lane, PE32 2XB.   T.755375. BB £ D2, T2. All year.
- G   Old Red Lion, Bailey Street, PE32 2AG. T.755557. www.oldredlion.here2stay.org.uk
BB £ to £++ F2, T2, D1. EM £7.50 - £10   Vegetarian wholefood menu.

Castle Acre (King's Lynn) Std 01760 (continued)

- G R   Willow Cottage Tea Rooms, Stocks Green, PE32 2AE. T.755551. BB £++ D2, T2. February-November. Snacks, teas and lunches.
- G   Rupert Guinness, 3 Stocks Green, PE32 2AE. T.755564. BB £+ D1, T1, S1. All year.
- S   Spar Shop & Post Office, Foxes Meadow, GR:817154. T.755274. Ecd Sunday

Brisley (Dereham) Std 01362 #

- G   Tully Lodge, School Lane, NR20 5LH. T./F.668493. BB £+ D1, T1. PWp

Great Massingham Std 01485

- S   PO/Shop. GR:798229. T.520272. Ecd Wednesday & Sunday.

Kings Lynn Std 01553. 12 miles (19kms) buses to Swaffham, Massingham & Hunstanton.

- Y   Youth Hostel, Thoresby College, College Lane, PE30 1JB. GR:616199. T.0870 770 5902. F./5903. 35 Beds (Open April - September - not every day)

Harpley (King's Lynn) Std 01485

- PH   Rose & Crown. GR:788258. T.520577. Food.
- G   Amanda Case, Lower Farm, PE31 6TU. GR:795260. T.520240. BB £++

Great Bircham (King's Lynn) Std 01485. 1.5 miles (2.4kms)

- R   Windmill Tearooms. GR:760326. T.578393. Mill. Stables. Cycle Hire. April - Sept. Wednesday - Sunday, plus Bank Holidays.
- H   Kings Head Hotel. GR:767322. T.578265. BB £++++ D2, T2, F1, S1. Food. Real ale.
- S   Country Store, Opposite Kings Head. Post Office in Church Lane

Sedgeford Std 01485

- PH   King William IV, Heacham Road. GR:710366. T.571765. Food. Real ale.
- G   Parkview, PE36 5LU. GR:711366. T.571352. BB £+, D1, T1, S1. EM £8. March - November.
- G   Eccles Cottage, Heacham Road. (close to PH) T.572688. BB £++ T1, S1. All year.
- S   Shop/PO by village green.

Ringstead Std 01485

- PH   Gin Trap, High Street. GR:706404. T.525264. Real ale. Food.
- C   Courtyard Farm, Ringstead. GR:729400. T.525251/526212. No regular campsite, phone for permission to camp at farm.
- BK   Courtyard Farm Bunkhouse Barn, PE365LQ. GR:729400. T.525369. Booking essential. 12 Bunk Beds, bring bedding and cooking equipment
- S   Ringstead Stores, High Street. GR:707406. Ecd Wednesday & Saturday
- R   Post Office Stores, High Street. T.525270

Hunstanton Std 01485. 3 miles (5kms) via Ringstead Downs & Lodge Farm. Ecd Thursday

- Y   Youth Hostel, 15 Avenue Road, PE36 5BW. GR:674406. T.0870 770 5872 F./5873 45 beds. Closed November -11th April & Sundays except July & August.
- G   Mrs B. Bamfield, The Gables, 28 Austin Street, PE36 6AW. T.532514. www.thegableshunstanton.co.uk BB £+/£++ D1,T1, F3. EM £13 6.30 pm. All year.
- G   Mr. N. Emsden, Sutton House Hotel, 24 Northgate, PE36 6AP. T.532552. mikeemsden@totalise.co.uk BB £++ D3, T2, F2, S1. EM All year.
- G   Mr. & Ms. Sturgess, Garganey House, 46 Northgate. PE36 6DR. T.533269. sturgess@garganey1fsnet..co.uk BB £+ D2, T2, S1, F1, EM £10 7.15 pm. All year
- G   Rosamaly Guest House, 14, Glebe Avenue, PE36 6BS. GR:675413. T.534187. www.rosamaly..co.uk BB £++ D3, T1, F2, S1, EM £11 5.30pm. All year except Xmas
- C   Searles Holiday Centre, South Beach. GR:671404. T.534211. 75 Tents £8 - £18. Mar-Novr.
- B S R   Barclays, NatWest, Nationwide. Food stores, supermarket. Fish and chips, cafes, restaurants.

Old Hunstanton Std 01485

- I   Neptune Inn, 85, Old Hunstanton Road. PE36 6HZ. T.532122. neptune-inn@supanet.com BB £++/£+++ D4, T1, F1. EM £15. Real Ale All year.
- H   Caley Hall Motel, PE36 6HH, T.533486. F.533348. BB £++++ 37 rooms
- G   Mrs Burton, 19 Wodehouse Road, PE36 6JW. T.532380. BB £++, D2, T1.
- G   Lesley Poore, Cobblers Cottage, 3 Wodehouse Road, PE36 6JD. T.534036. lesley.cobblerscottage@btinternnet.com BB £+/£+++ D1, T2. March-October.
- G   Lakeside, Waterworks Road. T./F.533763. BB £+++ D4, T2, S2. EM

Holme (Hunstanton) Std 01485

- S   GR:704435. 7 days. Lunch 1 - 2 pm closed.
- PH   White Horse, Kirkgate Street. GR:704435. T.525512. Food except Monday.
- G   Seagate House, Beach Road, PE36 6LG. T.525510. BB £++++ D1, T2.
- G   Mrs. Burton, Meadow Springs, 15, Eastgate. PE36 6LL. T.525279. BB £++ D1, T1.
- G   Mrs Simeone, Eastgates Cottage, Eastgate Road. PE36 6LL T.525218. BB £++++ T1.

Thornham (Hunstanton) Std 01485

- I   Lifeboat Inn, Ship Lane, PE36 6LT. GR:732435. T.512236. F.512323. www.lifeboatinn.co.uk reception@lifeboatinn.co.uk BB £++++ D4, T6, F3. Meals. Real ale. All year.
- H   Kings Head Hotel, High Street. PE36 6LY. GR:734434. T.512213. BB D4, S2. Bar Meals. Real ale.
- R   The Old Coach House, High St. T.512229. Pizza Café Bar, daily from 6pm, lunches Friday - Sunday
- G   Mr. M. Wyett, Rushmeadow, Main Road, PE36 6LZ GR:741434 T./F.512372. www.rushmeadow.com BB £++ D2, T1. No EM. All year.
- S R   Post Office, Stores, Bakery & Teashop. Opposite the church. T.512264

Titchwell (King's Lynn) Std 01485

- H   Titchwell Manor Hotel, PE31 8BB. GR:760437. T.210221. F.210104. www.titchwellmanor.co.uk margaret@titchwellmanor.co.uk BB £++++ D6, T6, F2, S1. Meals. Real ale. All year.
- H   Briarfields, Main Street, PE31 8BB. T.210742. F.210933 briarfields@norfolkhotels.co.uk www.norfolkhotels.co.uk BB £++++ D11, T4, F4. EM £10 All year.
- G   Mr. Pinder, 1, Main Road. GR:761437. T.210612. BB £+   D1. May – October.

Brancaster (King's Lynn) Std 01485

- I   Ship, Main Road. T.210333. GR:772439.   BB   D2, T1, F1. Meals. Real ale.
- G   John & Carol Symmington, Broadlane House, Broad Lane, T.210793. BB £+++ D2
- G   Mrs Townshend, The Old Bakery. T.210501. 400m. east of Ship. BB £+++ D2, F1.
- G   Mrs. Judy Rippon. T.210774
- S   Shops Ecd Wednesday, Sunday. Lunch: 1-2. GR:772437 & 774439.

Brancaster Staithe (King's Lynn) Std 01485

- I   The White Horse, Main Road. GR:800442. T.210262. BB £++++   D3, T5.
- PH   Jolly Sailors, Main Road. T.210314. GR:795444. Real Ale, Meals
- G   Redwings, Orchard Close, T.210459. BB £+++ T2.
- G   The Smithy (opp. Jolly Sailors) T.210638. BB £++ T1.
- G   Fiona Anderson, Apple Store Cottage. (close to Jolly Sailors) T.210331.   BB D1, T1.
- S   The Stores, Main Road. GR:800444. T.210338. Ecd Thursday, Sunday

Burnham Deepdale (King's Lynn) Std 01485

- Y C   Backpackers Hostel, PE31 8DD. T.210256. F.210158. www.deepdalegranary.co.uk 36 beds £ Bring bedding. Equipped kitchen. Camping all year. Granary Group Hostel, sleeps 18, can be booked as a whole.
- S PO   Deepdale Garage. Adjacent to Bunkhouse. Shop 7 days. T.210350

Burnham Market (King's Lynn) Std 01328 1.5 miles (2.4kms)

- **B S**   NatWest, Barclays. Various shops.
- **H**   The Railway Inn, Creake Road. T.730505.
- **PH**   Lord Nelson, Creake Rd. GR:835422. T.738321. info@lordnelsonburnhammarket.fsnet.co.uk F.738001. Real ale. Lunch. EM except Sunday -Tuesday. BB £+++ D2, F2.
- **H**   Hoste Arms, The Green, PE31 8HD GR:831422. T.738257. F.730103. www.hostearms.co.uk reception@hostearms.co.uk BB £++++ 28 rooms.
- **G**   Mrs L. Leftley, Wood Lodge, Herrings Lane, PE31 8DW. GR:830426. T.730152 F.730158. BB £+++ T2. No EM. All year except Xmas.
- **G**   Holmesdale, Church Walk. T.738699. veronicagroom@lineone.com £++ D1, T1. March - December
- **R**   Cafes, Fish & Chips

Burnham Overy Staithe (King's Lynn) Std 01328

- **PH**   Hero, Wells Road. GR:845443. T.738334. Real ale. Meals.
- **G**   Val Searle, The Brambles, (top of) Gong Lane, PE31 8JG. T.730273. BB £+++ T1.
- **G**   Mrs. Ann Smith, Domville House, Glebe Lane, PE31 8JQ. GR:846440. T.738298. BB £++ D2, T1, S1. EM £9.50 7.00pm. All year.

Holkham Std 01328 0.5 mile (0.8km)

- **H**   Victoria Hotel, Park Road. GR:891440. T.711008. BB F2, D6.
- **R**   Ancient House Tea Rooms. GR:892440. T.711285.

Wells-next-the-Sea Std 01328

- **Y**   Youth Hostel, Church Plain, NR23 1EQ. GR:917433. T.0870 770 6084. F./6085 31 beds. 16th April - 30th October, 2003
- **PH**   The Bowling Green Inn, opposite Church. T.710100. Real ale and food.
- **H**   Crown, The Buttlands. T.710209. F.711432. Real ale, food. BB £++++ All year.
- **I**   Lifeboat Inn, Station Road. T.710288. BB £++ D3, T1, S2. Meals. All year.
- **H**   Edinburgh Hotel, Station Road, NR23 1AE. GR:918435. T.710210. bubynum@hotmail.com BB £+/£++++ D1,T1, S1. EM £10 Real ale, food.
- **PH**   Globe Inn, The Buttlands. GR:916434. T.710206. Real ale, food.
- **PH**   Ark Royal, Freeman Street and Golden Fleece, The Quay. Real ale, meals.
- **B**   Barclays, 1 High Street. T.755500. Post Office, Station Road.
- **G**   East House, East Quay. GR:918436. T.710408. BB £++ D1, T2. January - November.
- **G**   Madeline Rainsford, The Old Custom House, East Quay, NR23 1LD. T.711463. F.710277. www.eastquay.co.uk BB £+++ D2, T1. All year except Xmas.
- **G**   Mrs J Court, Eastdene, Northfield Lane, NR23 1LH. GR:919436. T.710381. BB £++ D2, T1, S1. All year.
- **G**   The Normans, Invaders Court, Standard Road. T.710657. BB £++++ 5 rooms.
- **G**   Kilcoroon, Chancery Lane, NR23 1ER. T.710270. BB £++ D2, T1. Vegetarian.
- **G**   C & L Shayes, Meadowside, Two Furlong Hill, NR23 1HQ. GR:913433. T.710470. BB £+D1, T1. All year.
- **G**   Wingate, Two Furlong Hill. T.711814. BB £++ D2, T1.
- **G**   Brambledene, Warham Road. GR:922429. T.711143. BB £+ D2. November to September.
- **G**   Jean Whittaker, The Old Police House, Polka Road, NR23 1ED. GR:918434. T.710630. www.northnorfolk.co.uk/oldpolicehouse BB £++ D2, S1. All year.
- **G**   Crossways, 2, Park Road. GR:913435. T.711392. BB £+ D2, T1. All year
- **R**   Several cafes, restaurants and fish and chips along the Quay and Freeman Street
- **C**   Pinewoods Caravan and Camping Park, Beach Road, NR23 1DR. GR:914453. T.710439. www.pinewoods.co.uk 200 tents. Easter—December.

Warham Std 01328. 1:3miles (2km)
- PH   Three Horseshoes, The Street, NR23 1NL. T.710547. BB £++   D3, S1.   EM. Lunches Thursday to Saturday, real ale. All year

Stiffkey Std 01328
- C   Mr and Mrs Billings, 4 Greenway. GR:965438. T.830235. 75 tents. April to October.
- S   GR:972442. Seven days a week.
- PH   Red Lion, Wells Road. T.830552. Real ale, meals.
- G   The Saltings. GR:965434. T.830898

Morston (Holt) Std 01263.
- PH   Anchor Inn, The Street. GR:009439. T.740791. Food.
- G   Ned Hamond, Scaldbeck Cottage, Stiffkey Road, NR25 7BJ. T.740188. BB £++   D1, T1. eandnhamond@dialstart.net   www.glavenvalley.co.uk   February - November.

Blakeney Std 01263. Shops and PC at GR:027442.
- H   Blakeney Hotel, NR25 7NE. T.740797. BB £++++. Meals.
- I   White Horse, 4 High St. NR25 7AL. T.740574. F.741303. www.blakeneywhitehorse.co.uk Real ale, meals. BB   D6, F1, S2. All year.
- PH   King's Arms, Westgate Street. GR:026440. T.740341. Real ale, food, garden. BB
- G   Mrs M Image, Peartree Cottage, 81 High Street. T.741051. BB £+   T1. Summer only.
- G   Mrs Valentine, Anne Cottage, Back Lane. GR:031438 T.740760. BB   T1.
- G   Ryecroft, Back Lane, NR25 7NP. T.740701. BB £++   D1, T1. March to October.
- G   W & R Millard, White Barn, Back Lane, NR25 7NP (50m from main road) T./F.741359 Millard@clara.co.uk   http://members.tripod.co.uk/raymillard   BB £+++   D2, T1
- G   Navestock, Cley Road. (opp church). T./F.740998. BB £++++   D1, T1. February - December
- C   (2 miles south of Blakeney) Long Furlong Cottage Caravan Park, Blakeney Long Lane. GR:028414. T.740833/740266. Tents. No food. March to October

Wiveton Std 01263.1 mile (1:6km) off LDP at Cley
- PH   Bell, Blakeney Road. GR:042428. T.740101. Real ale, meals.

Cley-next-the-Sea Std 01263.
- H   George & Dragon, NR25 7RN. T.740652. Real ales, meals. BB £++++   D6, T1, F1. All year.
- I   Three Swallows, Newgate Green, Holt Rd. GR:047430. T.740526. BB £++ 6 rooms. Real ale, meals.
- GR   Cookes of Cley, Coast Road. T./F.740776.   BB £+++   D4, T2, F2. Lunch, EM.
- G   Cley Windmill, NR25 7NN. T.740209. BB   D1, T2, S1.
- G   Old Town Hall House, High Street, NR25 7RB. T./F.740284. BB £+++   D1, T2.
- G   Janet Panton, Droxford, Holt Rd, NR25 7OA. GR:045435. T.740440. BB £++   D1, T1. April - December.
- S R   Two shops and teashop in High Street, P.O. in Holt Road - closed lunch and Tuesdays p.m.

Salthouse (Holt) Std 01263
- PH   Dun Cow. GR 075439. T.740467. Real ale, food. 2 self contained flats.
- S   PO Stores. GR 075439. Ecd Wednesday, Saturday and Sunday. Closed 1-2pm.
- G   Mrs A Holman, Cumfus Bottom, Purdy St. NR25 7XA. T.741118. BB £++   D2, T1. All year.
- G   Springholes, Main Road, GR:079438. T.740307. BB £++   D1, T1.

Kelling Std 01263
- H   The Pheasant Hotel, Weybourne Road (A149) NR25 7EG. GR:098428. T.588382. F.588101. Real ale, all meals. BB £++++ 27 rooms.

Kelling Heath Std 01263
- C   Kelling Heath Holiday Park, NR25 7HW. GR:118415. T.588181. Caravans, 285 tents. April - October.

Weybourne Std 01263

H	Maltings Hotel, The Street. GR:110432. T.588731. BB 20 rooms, meals, real ale.
PH	Ship Inn. GR:110430. T.588721. Real ale, food, garden.
G	Home Farm, Holt Road, T.588334. BB £++ D2, T1.
G	The Stables, Bolding Way, T.588666. BB £++ D1, T1.
G	Millpeace, Sheringham Road, NR25 7EY. GR:115431. T.588655. BB £+ D2.
G	Sedgemoor, Sheringham Rd, NR25 7EY. GR:113429. T.588533. BB £ D2, All year.
S	Spar. GR:110431. Ecd Wednesday and Sunday. Closed lunch 1-2pm.

Sheringham Std 1263

Y	Youth Hostel, 1 Cremer's Drift, NR26 8HX. GR:159428. T.0870 770 6024 F./6025 100 beds. Open Fri-Sun 7th Feb-30th Nov, plus most school holidays (incl. half term).
H	The Two Lifeboats Hotel, 2 High Street, NR26 8JR. T.822401. F.823130. BB £++++ D3, T2, F2, S3. All year.
G	Mrs Meakin, Wykeham Guest House, Morley Road North, NR26 8JB. GR:158427. T.823818. BB £+ D1, T1, S1. April to October.
G	Melrose Hotel, 9 Holway Road. T.823299. BB £++ D3, T2, S1. All year
G	The Birches, 27 Holway Road. T.823550. BB £+++ T1, D1. April to October.
G	Holly Cottage, 14a The Rise. GR:162426. T.822807. BB £++ D1, T1. All year.
G	Bayleaf Guest House, 10 St Peter's Road. T.823779. F.820041. BB £+++ 7 rooms. No EM, 10% discount at local restaurants. All year.
G	Achimota, 31 North Street, NR26 8LW. T.822379. BB £+++ D1, T1.
G	Montague House, 3 Montague Road. T.822267. BB £++ 3 rooms. All year.
G	Willow Lodge, 6 Vicarage Road. T.822204. BB £+++ T4, F2. All year.
G	Mrs. D. North, Oakleigh, 31, Morris St. NR26 8JY. T.824993. dnorthoak@hotmail.com BB £+/£++ D1. EM £10 6.30pm. April to October.
G	Elmwood, 6, The Rise, NR26 8QA. T.825454. BB £+ D1, T1. All year except Xmas
GR	Whelk Coppers, Westcliff. T.825771. BB £+ D1, F1. Tearooms.
R	Craske's, High Street and others including fish and chips.
B	Barclays, HSBC, Natwest, Nationwide, etc.

West Runton (Cromer) Std 01263

G	Mrs. Power, Corner Cottage, Water Lane. T.838180. eddie@powerplans.co.uk. BB £++ D2,T1. All year.
G	Mrs K Elliott, Old Barn, Cromer Road. T.838285. BB £++ D1, T2.
C	Beeston Regis Camping Park, Cromer Road, West Runton. GR:174432. T.823614. 220 tents. March to October.
G	Homefield, Cromer Road. T.837337. BB £+++.

Aylmerton Std 01263

C	Roman Camp Caravan Park, NR25 9ND. GR:184414. T.837256. 10 tents.
I	Roman Camp Inn. GR:184406. T.838291. F.837071. BB £++++ D7, T8, EM.
G	Felbrigg Lodge. T.837588. F.838012. BB £++++ D3, T3. EM. All year.
G	Mrs J M Lee, Woodlands Guest House, Holt Road, NR11 8QA. GR:176408. T.837480. BB £+++ 6 rooms. All year.

East Runton   Std 01263
- C   Woodhill Park, Cromer Road. T.512242. Easter to October.
- S   Supermarket, butcher, post office.
- PH   White Horse and Fishing Boat. Both do meals, real ale.
- R   Berni's Social Club. Music, bar, snacks, fish and chips.
- C   Manor Farm. GR:199417 (camp site GR:204417). T.512858. April to October.

Cromer   Std 01263 Cabell Road is second on the left east of the rail station. Runton Road runs west along the front. Third on left is Macdonald Road with several guest houses.
- G   Birch House, 34 Cabell Road. T.512521.   BB £++   D4, T3, S1.   EM.
- H   Sandcliff Hotel, Runton Road. T./F. 512888. sandcliff@btclick.com. BB £+++ D7, T4, F10, S2. EM. All year.
- G   Glendale Guest House, 33 Macdonald Road, NR27 9AP. T.513278.   glendalecromer@aol.com BB £+   D2, T1, S2.
- H   Red Lion Hotel, Brooke Street. GR:220423. T.514964. BB £++++.
- G   Cambridge House, East Cliff, NR27 9HD. T.512085.   BB £++   D2, F3, S1.
- G   Mrs Votier, Morden House, 20 Cliff Avenue, NR27 0AN. GR:221417. T.513396. BB £+++   D4, T1, S1. EM. All year.
- C R   Sea Croft Camp Site, Runton Road, NR27 9NJ. GR:206 425. T.511722. 80 tents. Easter to October. Hillside Restaurant T.512315.
- B   Barclays, Abbey National, HSBC, Lloyds TSB, Natwest, etc.

Roughton   Std 01263   0.5 to 1.5 (0.8 to 2.4km) off the LDP.
- PH   New Inn, Norwich Road. GR:219368. T.761389 Meals
- R   Fish and chips, eat in or take away.
- S   Post office stores. GR:220371. Ecd Sunday.

Fellbrigg   Std 01263
- R   Fellbrigg Hall (National Trust). GR:193395. T.837444. Not open Thursdays & Fridays.

Aldborough   Std 01263
- S   Spar. Open 6 days plus am Sunday. Butcher, PO stores, ecd Wednesday, Saturday and Sunday
- PH   Black Boys, The Green. T.768086. Real ale, meals.
- R   The Old Red Lion, The Green. T.761451. Meals, 12-2pm and 7-9pm
- G   Butterfly Cottage, The Green, NR11 7AA. T.768198.   www.butterflycottage.com BB £++ D1, F1, T1, S1. All year.

Alby   Std 01263
- PH   Horseshoes, Cromer Road (A140). GR:207324. T.761378. Real ale, meals (handy for campsite below). PO at petrol station opposite.

Erpingham   (Norwich) Std 01263
- C   Little Haven, The Street. GR:203322. T.768959.   £8 per tent.   March to October.
- R   The Ark, GR:195322. T.761535.
- PH   Spread Eagle. GR:191319. T.761591. Real ale, food.

Calthorpe   (Norwich) Std 01263
- I R   Saracen's Head, Wolterton. GR:171323. T.768909. BB £++++   D2, T2. Lunch, EM, bar snacks, real ale.

Blickling   Std 01263
- PH   Buckinghamshire Arms (National Trust). GR:176286. T.732133. Real ale, bar meals, teas, EM.
- R   Blickling Hall House & Gardens (National Trust). 29th March - 2nd November 10.15 am to 5.15 pm. (House from 1 pm only). Closed Mondays, plus Tuesdays (except August).   Garden open Winter weekends 11 am -4 pm.   Restaurant open with garden. Park open all year.

Aylsham (Norwich) Std 01263 Shops. Most things are near the Market Place.
- B Post Office, Barclays, HSBC, Lloyds TSB, Alliance & Leicester.
- R Full Range - Fish & Chips, Cafes, Restaurants.
- PH Black Boys Inn, Market Place. T.732122. Real Ale. EM.   Feathers.   Unicorn.
- G Mrs. Jill Blake, Birchdale, Blickling Road, NR11 6ND. T.734531. www.smoothhound.co.uk/hotels/birchdale   BB £++ D2, T1, S1. All year.
- G The Old Pump House, Holman Road, NR11 6BY. T.733789.   BB £+ to £++   D3, T1, F1, S1. EM £15 by arrangement.   All year except Xmas.
- G The Old Manse, 43, Burgh Road. T.731283.   BB £+ D1, T1.
- G Mrs. Rowe, 10 Church Terrace, N R11 6EU. T.734319. BB £++   D1, T1.
- G Mrs. Bower, Old Mill House, Cawston Road. GR:186264. T.732118. BB £+ D1, T1.

Banningham Std 01263
- G Mrs. G. Harvey. Poplar Farm. North Walsham Rd. T.732680. BB £++   D2, T2.
- PH PO Crown Inn, Church Road. T.733534. Real ale. Meals

Felmingham Std 01692
- G Larks Rise. North Walsham Rd. T.403173. BB £++   F1 (sleeps 4).
- S Store & Post Office, North Walsham Rd. GR:250293. T.403340.

North Walsham Std 01692. Various Shops.
- B Barclays, HSBC, NatWest, Lloyds TSB, Alliance & Leicester, Norwich & Peterborough.
- H Kings Arms T.403054. F.500095. Real Ale. Meals. BB £++   D3, T2, S2.
- H Beechwood Hotel, 20, Cromer Rd. NR28 0HD.T.403231. F.407284, BB £++++   D9, T1. EM.
- PH Bluebell, Bacton Road.   Black Swan, Black Swan Loke. Both Real ale. Meals.
- PH Feathers.   White Swan. Orchard Gardens. All Real Ale.
- G Chimneys, 51, Cromer Road. GR:273306. T.406172. BB £++   D1, T1, F1.
- G Pinetrees, 45, Happisburgh Rd. T.404213.   BB £++ D1, T1. All Year.
- G Mrs. Millward, 25, Station Rd. T.403573. BB £+ D3, S1.
- G Mrs. Y .Mitchell, Green Ridges, 104 Cromer Road, NR28 0HE. T.402448. www.greenridges.com BB £+/£++   D1, T1, F1. EM £11 by arrangement. All year
- G Glaven Lodge, 26a, Bacton Road. NR28 9DR. GR:285304. T.404954.   BB £+   D2,T1. February - November.
- C Two Mills Touring Park , Yarmouth Rd. GR:2990287.   T.405829.

North Walsham Std 011692   On alternative route ,south of town at crossing of B1150. GR:278283.
- G The Toll Barn. T.403638. BB £++   D1, T1, S1. (continental breakfast).

Meeting House Hill   Std 01692. Phone box only facility.

Worstead (Norwich) Std 01692.   1 mile (2km) from Bengate on A149.
- I New Inn, Front Street. GR:302260. T.536296. Real Ale. Meals. BB£+   D2, T1.
- G The Ollands, Swanns Loke. T.535150. BB £++   D2, T1. EM. All Year.
- G Mrs. O'Hara, The Dyers House. (opp. church). T.536562.   BB £++   D1, T1, F1. EM.
- G Hall Farm, Sloley Rd. (1 km south of village). T.536124. BB £++ D1, T1, F1.

Honing Std 01692 Phone box only facility.

East Ruston   Std 01692.
- PH Butchers Arms. GR:345282. T.650237. Lunches, EM.

Stalham (Norwich) Std 01692.
- H — Kingfisher Hotel, High Street, NR12 9AN. T.581974. BB.£++++ D9, T3, F2, S4. Coffee, Lunches, EM. All year.
- PH — Swan Inn, High Street. T.581492. Real ale, Lunches & EM.
- PH — The Maids Head, The Grebe are both in the High street.
- B S R — Barclays, NatWest, variety of shops. Fish & chips take-away
- G — Sally Walsh, The Old Surgery, 137, High St. NR12 9BB. T.581248. durrellwalsh@aol.com BB £+ D1, T1, S1. All year except Xmas
- G — Gary & Beryl Holmes, Chapelfield Cottage. GR:369243. T.582173. BB£+++ D1, T1.
- G — Mrs. B. Mixer, Landell, Brick Kiln Lane, Ingham, NR12 9SX. GR:385256. T.582349 www.landell.co.uk BB £+ D1, T1. EM £12. All year except Xmas

Stalham Green (Norwich) Std 01692.
- PH — The Harnser. GR:382248. T.580347. BB++ Lunches & EM.

Sutton Std 01692.
- H — Sutton Staithe Hotel. T.560244. BB.
- S — PO GR:385237. Opposite Garden Centre up cul-de-sac. Ecd Wednesday.

Hickling Std 01692
- S — Hickling Stores. GR:410235. Ecd Wednesday, closed Sunday and 1-2pm.
- S — Newsagent & Post Office.
- PH — Greyhound, The Green. GR:410233. T.598306. Real ale. Snacks.
- G — Berties BB at the Greyhound. T.598306. BB £++ D1, T2, S1. Meals.
- PH — Pleasure Boat, Staithe Rd. GR:408225. T.598211. Real ale. Lunch & EM.
- G — Mrs. Froggatt, Paddock Cottage, Staithe Road. T.598259. BB £++ D2, F1.

Catfield Std 01692
- G — Mrs. Jill Wickens, Grebe Cottage, New Road, NR29 5BQ. GR:388218 T.584179 jill@wickens61.freeserve.co.uk BB £+ D2, T1. All year except Xmas
- PH — The Crown Inn, The Street. T.580128. BB £++ D1, T1. EM

Potter Heigham Std 01692.
- G — Mrs. Playford, Red Roof Farm. Ludham Road. T.670604. BB £+ D2, T1.
- S R — Post Office Stores. GR:415190. Shops, Fish & Chip Restaurant. GR:420185.
- I — Falgate Inn, Main Rd. GR:415190. T.670003. BB £++ D1, T2, F1, S2. Real ale. Lunch, EM.
- PH — Broads Haven Tavern, Bridge Rd. T.670329. Real ale. Lunch & EM.

Bastwick Std 01692.
- G — Mrs. J. Pratt, Grove Farm, GR:427177. T.670205
- S — Post Office. GR:423178. Ecd Saturday, closed Sunday. Garage, Spar, Off-licence.
- C — Mrs P Hunn, Whitehouse Camping, Main Road. GR:424180. T.670403. 20 pitches at £7 per night

Repps Std 01692.
- C — Willow Croft Camping Park, Staithe Road. T.670380. GR:414173. 30 pitches. £8.50 per night. Most of year.

Thurne Std 01692
- PH — Lion Inn, The Street. GR:403158. T.670196. Real ale. Meals.

Oby/Clippesby Std 01493.
- C — Bureside Holiday Park, Boundary Farm, Oby. GR:403152 T.369233.
- C — Clippesby Holidays. GR:422144 (1 mile-1.6km from route.) T.367800. May-September. Check beforehand at school holiday times

Acle Bridge Std 01493
- PH — Bridge Inn Tavern. GR:415116. T.750288. Real ale. Food.

Acle Std 01493
- PH — Kings Head, The Street. GR:402103. T. 750204. BB £+++ D3, T2, S1. Meals.
- R — Grumpys Restaurant, Fish & Chips. GR:402101. Chinese take away.
- I — East Norwich Inn, Old Rd, NR13 3QN nr. village centre. T.751109. F.751109. BB £++ Meals
- G — J & M Wallis, Old Police House, Reedham Road, NR13 3DE. GR:401101. T.751846. malcolm.wallis@btopenworld.com BB £+   D1, T1, S1. April to November.
- G R — Travel Lodge/Little Chef, NR13 3BE. A47/A1064 Roundabout, GR:405104. T./F.751970 (after 3 pm)   £44.95 for room sleeping 3 adults.
- B S — Barclays, T.634100. Lloyds TSB. T.750325. Shop GR:402104.
- PH — Riverside Inn. On The Old Yarmouth Rd. GR:409107. T.750310. EM (not Sunday).

Tunstall Std 01493.
- BK — Stone Barn. GR: 090409. 20 beds. Mrs. More, Manor Farm. NR13 3PS. T.700279. Book one day in advance by telephone.

Halvergate (Norwich) Std 01493
- PH — Red Lion, Marsh Rd. GR:424069. T.700317. Real ale. Lunch (not Sunday). No EM.
- G — School Lodge Country Guest House. Marsh Road, NR13 3QB T./F.700111. www.uk-guesthouse.com info@uk-guesthouse.com BB £+++   3 rooms EM.

Berney Arms Std 01493
- PH — Berney Arms. T 700303. Real ale. Meals. Open April to October.

Great Yarmouth Std 01493
- Y — Youth Hostel, 2 Sandown Road, NR30 1EY. GR:529083. T0870 770 5840 F./5841.   40 beds.
- G — Mr. Burth, Beaumont House, 52, Wellesley Road, NR30 1EX. GR:529080. T.843957. BB £+   D4, T2, S1, F2. EM £7. May to October.